Facilitator's Guide

Failure
Is NOT an
Option™

Six Principles That Guide

Student Achievement in

High-Performing Schools

Alan M. Blankstein

A Joint Publication of

CORWIN PRESS
A Sage Publications Company
Thousand Oaks, California

HOPE
Foundation

For information:

Corwin Press
A Sage Publications Company
2455 Teller Road
Thousand Oaks, California 91320
www.corwinpress.com

Sage Publications Ltd.
1 Oliver's Yard
55 City Road
London EC1Y 1SP
United Kingdom

Sage Publications India Pvt. Ltd.
B-42, Panchsheel Enclave
Post Box 4109
New Delhi 110 017 India

Printed in the United States of America.

ISBN 1–4129–3780–9

This book is printed on acid-free paper.

06 07 08 09 10   9 8 7 6 5 4 3 2

Acquiring Editor:	Faye Zucker
Editorial Assistant:	Gem Rabanera
Project Editor:	Astrid Virding
Typesetter:	C&M Digitals (P) Ltd.

Contents

About the Author

Alan M. Blankstein has worked within youth-serving organizations for 20 years, beginning as a music teacher. He subsequently worked for such organizations as the March of Dimes, Phi Delta Kappa, and the National Educational Service (NES), which he founded in 1987 and ran for 12 years. He has created award-winning publications and video staff development programs, including *Failure Is Not an Option*, the 2005 National Staff Development Council Book of the Year, *Reclaiming Youth At Risk*, and *Discipline With Dignity*; and he produced the PBS-ALSS and C-Span productions *Breaking the Cycle of Violence* and *Creating Learning Organizations: Growth Through Quality*.

Alan began the HOPE Foundation (Harnessing Optimism and Potential Through Education) as a nonprofit organization whose Honorary Chair is Archbishop Desmond Tutu. HOPE supports educational leaders over time in creating school cultures in which all students succeed, especially underserved students. Alan and the HOPE staff began their work around "quality" and "professional learning communities" in 1988 by bringing W. Edwards Deming and his work to light in educational circles through a series of Shaping America's Future forums and videoconferences that involved Al Shanker, Peter Senge, Mary Futrell, Linda Darling-Hammond, Ed Zigler, the CEOs of Firestone, GM, and Ford, and scores of other leaders. The HOPE Foundation provides support for some 10,000 leaders annually through Courageous Leadership Institutes, Courageous Leadership Academies, and Comprehensive School Reform based on the Failure Is Not an Option Learning Communities of HOPE.

Based on his own background as a "youth at risk" growing up in New York and on his professional career in education, Alan has authored the *Reaching Today's Youth Curriculum*, now provided as a course in 16 states; and he has written articles for *Educational Leadership, The School Administrator, Executive Educator, High School*

Magazine, and *Reaching Today's Youth.* In addition, Alan provides keynote presentations and staff development, reaching tens of thousands of professionals annually through organizations including the Association for Supervision and Curriculum Development (ASCD), the National Association of Secondary School Principals (NASSP), National Association of Private Schools for Exceptional Children, Illinois Council of Administrators for Exceptional Children, and the International Association of Special Educators.

How to Use This Chapter-by-Chapter Guide

*"**Failure Is Not an Option** addresses all the elements that are absolutely necessary for effective and enduring educational reform. It is a deeply passionate call to arms, combined with the wherewithal to take systematic, continuous, and effective action. A must read for all those interested in reform because it is simultaneously inspiring and practical."*

—From the *Failure Is Not an Option* Foreword by Michael Fullan, former Dean, Ontario Institute for Studies in Education, University of Toronto

This Facilitator's Guide is a companion to *Failure Is Not an Option™: Six Principles That Guide Student Achievement in High-Performing Schools,* a book that tells the vivid story of what it takes to turn schools around, continually improve schools that are already good, and succeed with ALL students. Drawing on 15 years of practical research, and an in-depth look at 20 high-performing schools and districts, the book identifies six principles that guide sustainable professional learning communities. Most important, readers will find a detailed set of field-tested processes for re-creating these successes in their own schools.

Many schools are choosing this accessible publication for collaborative book study groups. Most groups will read one or two chapters (usually about 30–40 pages) before each group meeting. This simple guide is structured to help the leader facilitate those meetings.

For each meeting, a set of **reading and review questions** will help readers prepare for the group meeting by highlighting the main points of each chapter. Readers may want to write down answers to the questions and take them to the group meeting.

Suggested group **activities** are designed for small or large groups but can be undertaken by individuals working alone. In advance of each meeting, decide which activities you will be pursuing together and which activities members will be encouraged to do on their own.

The **open-ended discussion questions** are designed to encourage members both to apply what they have read to their own experiences or current professional concerns and to share these with their colleagues. In some cases you may want to look at the discussion questions first and then undertake the activities, or you may want to alternate between activities and discussion. In every case, the activities and discussion questions are meant to be suggestions only. Each group leader may decide to skip some, add others, or amend all to fit local issues.

Finally, there are suggestions for **further reading** for practitioners who wish to pursue a topic in greater depth individually or for group members to assign in round-robin fashion so that each member reads and summarizes a selection during the series of meetings.

Note: Chapter 5 is longer and more complex than the others. You may want to schedule extra time for the meeting at which it is discussed, or discuss it over two successive meetings.

Tips to Facilitate Discussion

- Read the material in advance and budget time for each portion of the study.

- Use a model of team facilitation. Two facilitators can keep the conversation interesting, and each often engages the study group in different ways. In addition, expand the opportunity for leadership to include everyone who is willing to lead.

- Use a full range of visual aids. Instead of having participants write on paper only, use an overhead projector, computer, flip chart, marker board or other tools. Ask participants to help.

- If your study is not done in a single session but rather extends over a period of time, get contact information for all participants and communicate with them between study dates. This can be useful to remind participants of the next study and to refresh their memory of the previous topics discussed.

- For ongoing study, create a space on the Internet or intranet where participants can add comments and collaborate.

- Send participants study questions and meeting details in advance.

- Select a location that is comfortable, such as a participant's home or casual meeting room. A location other than school can be more inviting and contribute to a better meeting experience.

- Include light refreshments as an extra feature for a meeting. Serve the refreshments at different times during the meeting. Participants can contribute.

- Make the study relevant to the group's experiences. You do not have to limit the discussion to the questions in the study guide.

- Take a break during the meeting for personal conversations.

- Do an opening ice breaker. It helps start a more relaxing meeting.

- Take time to reflect and summarize at the conclusion of the meeting.

- If several participants in the study have been too busy to read the book in advance, consider allowing some time at the beginning of the meeting for them to read the selected material.

- Collect filled-in Evaluation Forms from the participants at the conclusion of the meeting and use their comments for ongoing improvement of future meetings.

CHAPTER 1: WHY *FAILURE IS NOT AN OPTION*

Review of Chapter Content

Name two primary reasons why failure is not an option in education.

Activity

In a statement of no more than two sentences, complete the following: "I decided to become an educator because. . . ." Share and discuss your response with others in your study group. You may want to form smaller groups of two or three for this activity.

Discussion

The author poses the question, "Why are we in this profession?" (pp. 4–5). Why, according to him, is this question key to any successful improvement effort?

CHAPTER 2: COURAGEOUS LEADERSHIP FOR SCHOOL SUCCESS

Review of Chapter Content

1. The author defines the "Courageous Leadership Imperative" as "acting in accordance with one's own values, beliefs, and mission" (p. 15). Explain what the author means by this definition.

2. List the five axioms characterizing courageous leadership.

Activity

On pp. 21 and 22, three activities are suggested that can help leaders reflect on their core values and ideals. As a group, decide in advance which one(s) you will undertake and whether you will attempt the activity alone before your next meeting (e.g., the three listed questions on p. 22) or together as a group (the activities involving pairs and triads suggested on p. 21).

Discussion

1. How do you respond to the idea that the education of the young is a moral issue?

2. Respond to the following statement: "Leaders who overturn long-held assumptions and traditions to direct their schools and students toward a better future often face strong resistance in school, district, and larger community."

3. From your own experience, what are some reasons why leading change requires courage?

4. What might help skeptical, cynical, or burned-out educators recoup the idealism that led most of them into the profession at the beginning of their careers?

Further Reading

Darling-Hammond, L. (1997/2001). *The right to learn: A blueprint for creating schools that work.* San Francisco: Jossey-Bass.

Evans, R. (1996). *The human side of school change.* San Francisco: Jossey-Bass.

Fullan, M.G. (2003). *The moral imperative of school leadership.* Thousand Oaks, CA: Corwin Press.

Glickman, C. (2003). *Holding sacred ground: Essays on leadership, courage, and endurance in our schools.* San Francisco: Jossey-Boss.

CHAPTER 3: TEN COMMON ROUTES TO FAILURE, AND HOW TO AVOID EACH

Review of Chapter Content

1. List (mentally or on paper) six reasons TQM failed to improve many schools (pp. 40–44) and four additional reasons such reform efforts fail.

2. Cite examples of ways the Alton School District and Nancy Duden overcame these barriers to progress.

Activity

1. Complete the self-assessment (Appendix A) on pp. 215–216. (District administrators might answer in terms of the district as a whole.) Discuss your ratings with other members of the group. Is there a consensus in your group about some of the negative ratings?

2. Review the list of "Strategies for Making Time" (Appendix B) on pp. 219–220. Then, in groups of three or four, brainstorm additional strategies and discuss ways that some of these strategies could be implemented in your schools.

Discussion

1. Recall any improvement efforts you have been involved with or have witnessed. Share these experiences with other group members. How did the obstacles listed on pp. 40–47 affect the improvement efforts under discussion?

2. Review the "Strategies for Dealing With Resistance" (Appendix C) on pp. 221–222. Share and discuss incidents when the listed "ineffective behaviors" (p. 221) demolished well-designed improvement initiatives.

3. Recall and share situations in which you encountered resistance to a change or improvement you espoused, or describe a planned change that is likely to arouse resistance. How could the use of any of the strategies listed on p. 222 affect your chances of implementing the change?

Further Reading

Blankstein, A. M., & Swain, H. (1994, February). Is TQM right for schools? *The Executive Educator, 51.*

Fullan, M. G. (2001). *Leading in a culture of change.* San Francisco: Jossey-Bass.

Fullan, M. G. (2004). *Leading in a culture of change: Personal action guide and workbook.* New York: John Wiley.

CHAPTER 4: BUILDING A PROFESSIONAL LEARNING COMMUNITY WITH RELATIONAL TRUST

Review of Chapter Content

1. Review the formulations on which the concept of the "learning community" is founded (Figure 4.1, p. 55). Compare these with the six principles proposed by the author on p. 56.

2. Articulate the concept or definition of "community" that characterizes an ideal school community.

3. Define "relational trust" and list its four components.

Activity

1. Read the "Teacher-Principal Trust Item" (Appendix J) on p. 257 and apply it to your school. Mark each item N (Never), S (Sometimes), or A (Always). (If your group consists of administrators rather than teachers, change the word "principal" to "superintendent" and "school" to "district" in each item.) Discuss the results with other group members.

2. In small groups, look over the items in the shaded box on p. 50 and analyze each to show how the described situation reflects, or is founded on, a trusting interpersonal relationship. (You may skip the item about SMART goals, which will be taken up in the next chapter.) Consider whether the same situations would be found in your own school(s).

Discussion

1. Consider, in turn, each of the six principles that the author proposes as the "essence" of a professional learning community (p. 56). What, if anything, do you believe may have been left out? List any suggested omissions. After you have finished the book, decide whether those items you thought were missing were subsumed under one of the principles discussed in the remaining chapters.

2. Discuss instances in which talented administrators (superintendents or principals) failed to gain the trust of those working under them. What were some elements in personal relationships that led to this failure? (Discuss and rate the actions of the leaders against the list of components in Figure 4.4 on p. 62.)

Further Reading

Barth, R. S. (2001). *Learning by heart.* San Francisco: Jossey-Bass.

Bryk, A. S., & Schneider, B. (2002). *Trust in schools: A core resource for improvement.* New York: Russell Sage.

Hargreaves, A. (2003). *Teaching in the knowledge society.* New York: Teachers College Press.

Learning Communities—What Do They Look Like and How Do You Get There? *School Administrator* 5:60 (May 2003).

CHAPTER 5: PRINCIPLE #1–COMMON MISSION, VISION, VALUES, AND GOALS

Review of Chapter Content

1. Name the "four pillars of any organization"—the foundation blocks of its culture—and define each.

2. Describe one or two ways to implement each of the four pillars.

Activity

Note: Depending on the time available, you may want to form small groups, each ideally comprised of staff from the same school or from the same school level (e.g., elementary or middle schools). Each group might focus on one of the following activities, or, as this chapter is quite lengthy, use two group meetings to address the activities and questions below.

1. Review the three questions listed on p. 67 and the content of Figure 5.1 on p. 73. With these questions and characteristics in mind, critique your own school's or district's mission statement(s). Then, look at the bulleted items on p. 76. How many of the listed strategies for keeping your mission statement alive are you currently using? List any other strategies you can think of.

2. Read and consider the "Think It Through . . ." questions on p. 84. If your school or district has a vision statement, critique it using the criteria on p. 78 and the general characteristics in Figure 5.2 on p. 80. If your organization has no vision statement, write statements that you might include if you were asked to write one.

3. Discuss, define, and list the values implicit in your school's or district's culture. If you have existing mission and vision statements, refer to them. Examine each implicit value that you list by asking, "Is this value consistent with our mission? Will this value help us realize our vision?"

4. Review the characteristics of SMART goals (p. 91). Review goals that your school or district has adopted and decide whether they are SMART.

Discussion

1. In small or large groups, discuss whether you need to rewrite or revitalize your mission, vision, values, or goals. Decide what steps need to be taken to begin the process.

2. While reviewing the bulleted items on pp. 92–93, discuss the kinds of events and achievements that are typically celebrated in your school(s). Should you rethink your policies and start celebrating other kinds of successes? Where should you begin?

Further Reading

Barth, R. (2001). *Learning by heart.* San Francisco: Jossey-Bass.

DuFour, R., & Eaker, R. (1998). *Professional learning communities at work: Best practices for enhancing student achievement.* Bloomington, IN: National Educational Service.

Hord, S. M. (2003). *Learning together, leading together: Changing schools through professional learning communities.* New York: Teachers College Press and Oxford, OH: National Staff Development Council.

CHAPTER 6: PRINCIPLE #2–ENSURING ACHIEVEMENT FOR ALL STUDENTS: SYSTEMS FOR PREVENTION AND INTERVENTION

Review of Chapter Content

1. Name "three common reasons" that school communities fail to take responsibility for ensuring that *all* children learn, and suggest ways of addressing these.

2. List some traditional ways of "diagnosing" problem students and dealing with their misbehavior. Describe the basis of the Community Circle of Caring's alternative approach.

3. Describe the four components of a comprehensive system for assuring the success of all students.

Activity

1. In small groups, preferably comprising staff at the same school or at the same grade level range (e.g., all middle school), answer the questions on the worksheet (Appendix F) on pp. 235–236.

2. Form at least four small groups. Each group should sketch out a plan for answering the questions under one of the four topics in Appendix G on pp. 237–238 (identification, monitoring, mentoring, and intervention). Begin work on each topic by listing programs already in place and discussing their adequacy.

Discussion

1. Characterize the prevailing beliefs of your colleagues and staff about the power of teachers to ensure that all students are successful. How has staff behavior that reflects these beliefs affected student achievement, for better or for worse?

2. The following question is in "Think It Through . . ." on p. 101: "How do leaders respond to behaviors that conflict with vision, mission, and values?" How would you answer that question?

3. Review Figure 6.5 on p. 111. Which column describes the practices in your school(s)? What can you do to ensure that your policies fall in the left-hand column?

Further Reading

Blankstein, A. M., DuFour, R., & Little, M. (1997). *Reaching today's students.* Bloomington, IN: National Educational Service.

Darling-Hammond, L., & Bransford, J. (Eds.). (2005). *Preparing teachers for a changing world: What teachers should learn and be able to do.* San Francisco: Jossey-Bass.

Evans, R. (1996). *The human side of school change.* San Francisco: Jossey-Bass.

CHAPTER 7: PRINCIPLE #3–COLLABORATIVE TEAMING FOCUSED ON TEACHING AND LEARNING

Review of Chapter Content

1. Describe characteristics of a culture of collaboration and list areas in which such teaming may occur.

2. List some of the protocols for teamwork that need to be decided for effective collaboration.

3. Name some challenges to creating a collaborative culture and ways these can be addressed.

Activity

1. Consider the meetings of your study group for this book. Are there protocols you could establish to make your meetings more productive and useful? In small groups, draw up a set of "rules" for the rest of your meetings. Share these with the group and decide which of them you will observe from now on.

2. Consider a problem affecting your school or district that could be addressed by an effective team that is interdisciplinary (within a single school) or across two or more schools. Draw up a proposal for such a team that includes a list of its members, its goal or purpose, the logistics of its meeting and timeframe, and the responsibilities of its members.

Discussion

1. Consider the "Think It Through . . ." questions on p. 135. How would you answer them?

2. How can collaboration among teachers lead to a sharing of the instructional strengths of each of them?

3. Discuss ways that teams of middle and high school representatives can improve student learning and preparedness for high school work.

Further Reading

Fullan, M., & Hargreaves, A. (1996). *What's worth fighting for out there?* New York: Teachers College Press.

Roberts. S. M., & Pruitt, E. Z. (2003). *Schools as professional learning communities: Collaborative activities and strategies for professional development.* Thousand Oaks, CA: Corwin Press.

CHAPTER 8: PRINCIPLE #4–USING DATA TO GUIDE DECISION MAKING AND CONTINUOUS IMPROVEMENT

Review of Chapter Content

1. Name the kinds of data that should be collected, several ways that collected data can be used effectively, and who should review, analyze, and use them.

2. Describe characteristics of data that are useful for planning school improvement and ways that the collected data can be used.

3. List several obstacles or challenges to collecting, analyzing, and using data effectively and ways these can be confronted or resolved.

Activity

1. Review the case history beginning on p. 159. In small groups, brainstorm lists of the kinds of data you might collect from your school(s) or district.

2. For each item on your list, determine the best ways to obtain the information you want (e.g., survey, focus groups, interviews, test scores, and so forth) or the sources of data that are currently available.

Discussion

1. What data would you need to collect in order to determine the causes of poor reading scores among third graders?

2. In your opinion, how well do results of state tests reflect the quality of student learning? If you feel there is a discrepancy, what are some kinds of data you can collect or generate to determine what skills and knowledge the students have actually acquired?

3. Read and discuss the "Think It Through" question on p. 152. If you accept the idea that high average scores may be masking some students' serious problems, what data will you collect, and how will you analyze or disaggregate them?

Further Reading

McTighe, J., & Wiggins, G. (2004). *Understanding by design: Professional development workbook.* Alexandria, VA: Association for Supervision and Curriculum Development.

Reeves, D. B. (2000a). *Making standards work* (3rd ed.). Denver, CO: Advanced Learning Press.

CHAPTER 9: PRINCIPLE #5–GAINING ACTIVE ENGAGEMENT FROM FAMILY AND COMMUNITY

Review of Chapter Content

1. Name three key principles of positive school-family relationships and examples of each.

2. List the National PTA's six standards for family involvement and examples of each.

3. Name several challenges or obstacles to establishing good ties between school and community and possible solutions for each.

Activity

1. In small groups, read and discuss the scenarios in the boxed section, "What Good Looks Like" on pp. 177–179, rating each on the quality of the interaction and giving reasons why it deserves such a rating.

2. In small groups, draw three columns on a piece of paper. In the first column, list typical issues involving family responsibilities for their children's schooling (tardiness, absenteeism, incomplete homework, failure to sign homework or other forms, etc.). Next to each, note the school's current policy in regard to the issue. In the third column, note possible reasons for the problem. Discuss whether the established policies address the source of the problem effectively, and what a more empathetic approach might involve.

Discussion

1. Discuss and rate the quality of your school's or district's relationship with the community. What particular policies or practices could be adopted by schools that do not have positive ties?

2. Share and discuss experiences of group members or their colleagues in attempting to reach out to, or draw in, family and community members. In cases where these efforts were unsuccessful or frustrating, what might have been done differently?

3. How do you respond to the idea of making school representatives more visible at community gathering places and events?

Further Reading

Elias, M. J., et al. (2003). *Challenges in creating effective home-school partnerships in adolescence: Promising paths for collaboration*. Chicago: Collaborative for Academic, Social, and Emotional Learning.

National PTA. (1997). *National standards for parent/family involvement*. Chicago: National PTA. http://www.pta.org/archive_article_details_1118251710359.html

CHAPTER 10: PRINCIPLE #6–BUILDING SUSTAINABLE LEADERSHIP CAPACITY

Review of Chapter Content

1. Explain why building leadership capacity in a school or district should be a priority concern.

2. Name and define six different leadership styles.

3. Describe several different ways that teachers can act as leaders.

4. Define or describe *sustainability* of leadership in educational institutions, and the role of instructional leadership, "distributed" leadership, and leadership succession.

Activity

1. List instances in your school(s) or district in which teachers played leadership roles (e.g., obtaining grants for instructional initiatives; organizing professional study groups, mentoring programs, or other professional development activities; evaluating or developing curricula or local assessments, and so on). Brainstorm ways these teachers can be encouraged and supported in their efforts so that others may be encouraged to exercise similar leadership.

2. Using the definitions in Figure 10.1 on p. 195, have administrators or others in leadership roles in the group silently evaluate their own leadership styles and consider approaches to raise the style to an even more positive level. If they feel comfortable, they could discuss their self-evaluations with colleagues.

Discussion

1. Share experiences of improvement initiatives that floundered when leaders left. In retrospect, suggest steps the original leaders

might have been taken to ensure that the impetus for change was sustained.

2. If your group consists largely of administrators, share and discuss your reactions to the idea of sharing leadership and responsibility with teaching staff. If the group is composed of teachers, discuss the kinds of instructional or professional development leadership opportunities you would like to initiate, and the kinds of support (time or other resources) you would require to do so.

Further Reading

Collins, J. (2001). *Good to great.* New York: HarperCollins.

Huffman, J. B., & Hipp, K. K. (2004). *Reculturing schools as professional learning communities.* Lanham, MD: Scarecrow Education.

WRAP UP YOUR READING WITH REFLECTION

When you have completed the series of group meetings or workshops on the chapters of *Failure Is Not an Option,* answer the following questions and then take time as a group to celebrate your hard work and mastery of school improvement theory and practice.

1. What is the most valuable lesson your school or district has learned from reading and discussing the book with your colleagues?

2. In light of what you have learned, what should be the two highest priority actions for improvement in your school or district?

3. What actions will you, individually or with colleagues, take as a result of what you have learned?

4. Sketch out a possible timeline for the actions you listed in answering Questions 2 and 3.

5. What, if any, follow-up activities would you like your group to undertake?

6. What have you learned about collaboration and teamwork as a result of the activities and discussions in this guide?

   a. What did you like about this process?

   b. What would you do differently if you were to do this again?

7. Set a date to get back together to exchange what you've done. Identify how the group can help you as a result of your experience in applying this reading to your practice.

EVALUATION FORM

The facilitator(s) can choose one or two questions from each category to make up an evaluation form. This form can be adapted for each chapter, workshop, or study group meeting.

Content

- How well did the meeting, workshop, or seminar meet the goal and objective?

- How will you apply what you have learned today to your daily professional life?

- What professional support will you need to implement what you have learned today?

- How well did the strategies or topics explored today meet a specific need at your school site or in your district?

- How relevant was this meeting, workshop, or seminar to your professional life?

Process

- How well did the instructional techniques and activities facilitate your understanding of the topic?

- How will the activities presented today help your future teaching?

- Was any particular activity memorable? What made it stand out?

- What areas of today's topic still need exploration/clarification for you to assimilate the knowledge into your daily professional life?

Context

- Were the physical facilities conducive to learning?

- Were the accommodations adequate for the activities involved?

- Were adequate lighting, comfortable chairs, and refreshments available?

Overall

• Overall, how successful would you consider this meeting, workshop, or seminar to be in helping you become a more reflective practioner? Please include a brief comment or explanation.

• What was the most valuable idea you gained from this meeting, workshop, or seminar?

Note: Adapted from *Evaluating Professional Development* by Thomas R. Guskey, Thousand Oaks: Corwin Press, 2000.

CORWIN PRESS

The Corwin Press logo—a raven striding across an open book—represents the union of courage and learning. Corwin Press is committed to improving education for all learners by publishing books and other professional development resources for those serving the field of PreK–12 education. By providing practical, hands-on materials, Corwin Press continues to carry out the promise of its motto: **"Helping Educators Do Their Work Better."**

The HOPE Foundation logo stands for Harnessing Optimism and Potential Through Education. The HOPE Foundation helps to develop and support educational leaders over time at district- and state-wide levels to create school cultures that sustain all students' achievement, especially low-performing students.